silly Millies

Beach Riddles

Jennie Spray Doering
illustrated by Steve Pica

Millbrook Press • Minneapolis

To Emmie and Nattie,
for always laughing
at my jokes (or else!)

Millbrook Press, Inc.
A division of Lerner Publishing Group
241 First Avenue North
Minneapolis, Minnesota 55401 U.S.A.

Website address: www.lernerbooks.com

Library of Congress Cataloging-in-Publication Data

Doering, Jennie Spray.
Beach riddles / by Jennie Spray Doering ; Illustrated by Steve Pica.
p. cm. — (Silly Millies)
ISBN-13: 978–0–7613–2885–8 (lib. bdg. : alk. paper)
ISBN-10: 0–7613–2885–8 (lib. bdg. : alk. paper)
1. Riddles, Juvenile. 2. Sea—Juvenile humor. I. Pica, Steve, ill. II. Title.
III. Series.
PN6371.5.D53 2007
818'.602—dc22 2005032445

Printed in China
2 3 4 5 6 7 – LP – 12 11 10 09 08 07

What's the friendliest way to start a day at the beach?

The high and low tides change with the cycles of the moon.

What did the baby whale say while heading south?

Whales travel in groups called pods,
much like fish travel in schools.

Where's the best place to go shopping at the beach?

On a *sail*boat!

When you do go shopping,
don't forget your sand dollars!

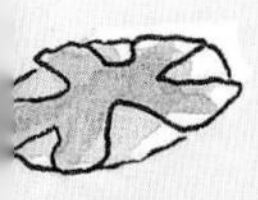

Sand dollars are living animals. If you find one that looks like it has tiny hairs on it, put it back! It's still alive.

Did you hear about the whale pirate?

Plankton is the "soup" of the sea, made of very, very tiny animals and plants. Whales and many other animals eat plankton.

He made his prisoners
walk the *plank*-ton!

Who keeps the ocean floor clean?

Mer-*maids*.

Who fixes things
in the ocean?

*Hammer*head sharks.

Sharkskin is covered with tiny, teeth-like points.
Don't pet a shark the wrong way!

Who's in charge of ocean soccer games?

The *reef*-eree.

Which team wins ocean soccer?

Nobody. The score is always *tide*!

A reef is a huge rocky shape made by millions of tiny animals called coral polyps.

Who plays the
best ocean music?

Orcas are also called killer whales because of their fierce hunting skills.

Which sea creature sings the best?

The *choral* polyps.

Coral polyps don't really sing,
but they do make giant reefs.

Which fish is the best fighter?

The *sword*fish!

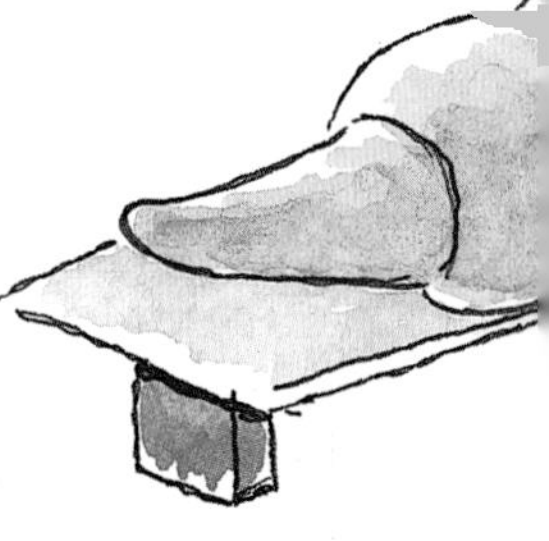

When a swordfish is young, it doesn't have a sword. As it grows up, it's upper jaw grows longer and longer until it has its sword.

But mollusks are more dangerous.

They've got more *mussels*!

Mollusks are soft animals that often—but not always—live in a hard shell. Mussels, clams, and conches are all types of mollusk.

Who are the best fliers?

The *pilot* fish.

Pilot fish don't really fly. They got their name from their habit of swimming along with sharks and whales, as if they are piloting them.

Why aren't fish good gardeners?

Too many sea*weeds*.

Seaweeds are actually a very important part of the ocean's ecosystem, much like plants on land.

How can you tell a squid from an octopus?

Count his *ten*tacles.

An octopus has eight arms, but a squid has ten. Two of the squid's arms are longer than the rest and are used to grab onto its prey.

Where do ocean animals sleep?

In Kelp *beds*.

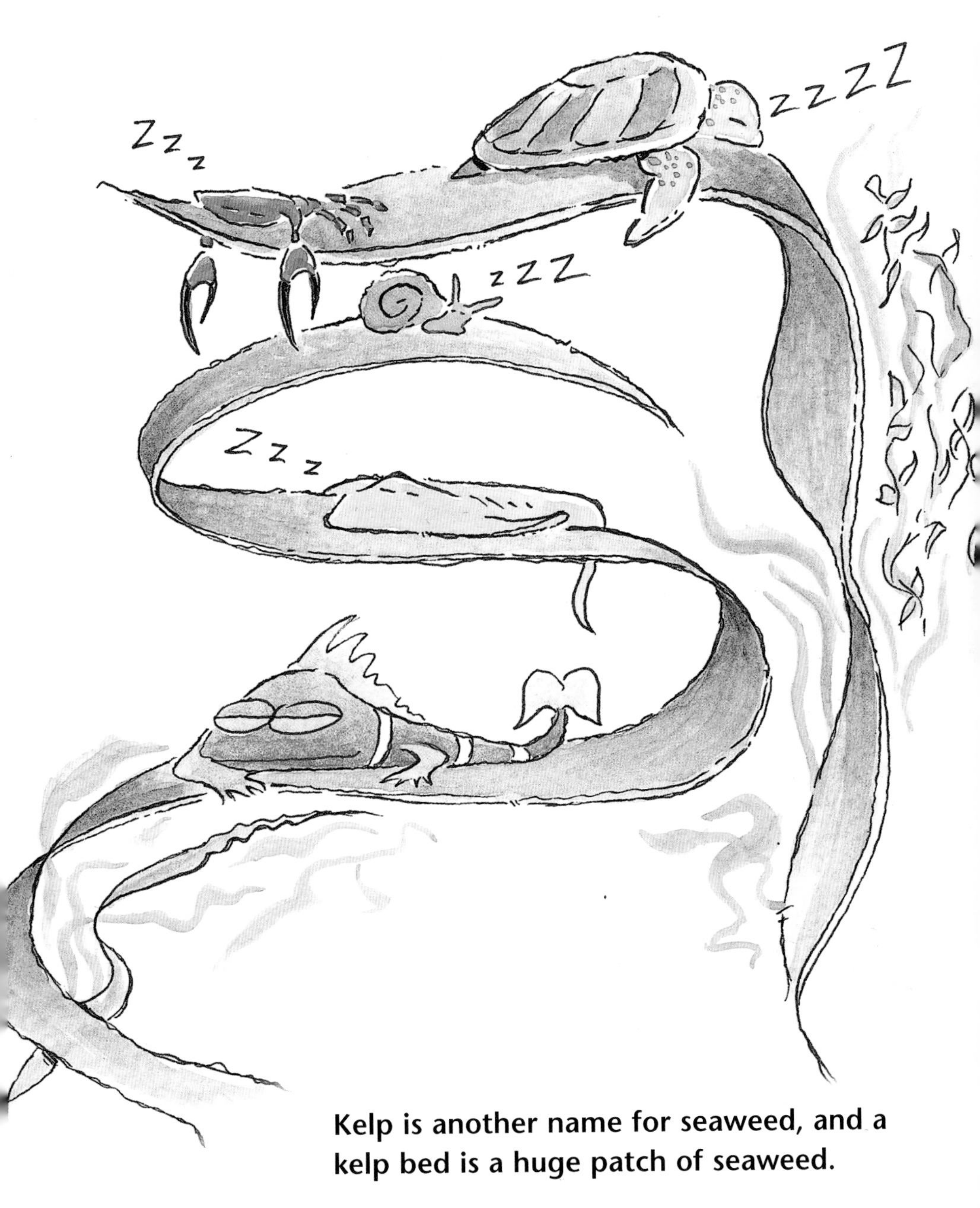

Kelp is another name for seaweed, and a kelp bed is a huge patch of seaweed.

What fish only comes out at night?

The starfish, or sea star, is not a fish, but an echinoderm, which means "hedgehog skin." If it loses an arm, it can grow another one in its place.

And when you leave the beach . . .

wave **good-bye!**

Tips for Discussion

- A homophone is one of two or more words that are pronounced the same but have different spellings and different meanings—for example, pare, pear, and pair. There are five riddles based on homophones in this book. The first one is on page 3—high and hi. Can you find the other four pairs of homophones?
- If two words are pronounced the same and spelled the same but have different meanings, they are known as homonyms. Can you identify the homonym on page 31?
- Can you make up your own riddle about the beach? The terms *school of fish* or *sandbank* might give you some ideas.

About the Author

Jennie Spray Doering lives in Tempe, Arizona, but heads out to the beach whenever she can. She loves the ocean as much as she loves telling jokes and was thrilled to combine both in her first book. She has two kids, three cats, and a newly minted Master of Fine Arts degree from Vermont College in Writing for Children and Young Adults.